Believe in your Swing!
KB

Copyright © 2015 by Kevin Braun and Jordan Dunseth
All rights reserved. This book or any portion thereof
may not be reproduced or used in any manner whatsoever
without the express written permission of the publisher
except for the use of brief quotations in a book review.

Printed in the United States of America

First Printing, 2015

ISBN 978-0-692-56296-3

www.10andUnderTennisBook.com

A is for "Ace"

When the tennis ball is served in and not touched by the receiver.

B is for "Backhand"

Set the Racquet: Keeping your arms parallel to the baseline, with the racquet head above your hands, you set the racquet in position to hit the ball.

Turn Your Shoulders: Rotate your shoulders so that your arms are perpendicular to the baseline, making sure your racquet does not rotate to the opposite side of the body.

Let the Racquet Drop: Prior to the forward portion of the swing, the racquet head will drop from above the hands to below the hands.

Pull the String: Pretending there is a string tied to the bottom of the racquet, the string will be pulled toward the ball.

Turn the Doorknob: After making contact with the ball, the racquet will go from the hitting side to the non-hitting side of your body; like your hand is turning a doorknob.

Show Your Elbows: A completed swing will result in your elbows pointing toward your target.

C is for "Crosscourt"

Hitting the ball from one corner of the court to the opposite corner.

D is for "Down the Line"

When a ball is hit straight along the sideline to the opponent's side of the court.

- Even if you're not playing well, you should always have a good attitude. Smile, it's just a game!
- Play at the pace of the server; don't intentionally slow down the game
- If a ball from another court rolls onto your court, stop play and re-start the point

F is for "Forehand"

Set the Racquet: Keeping your arms parallel to the baseline, with the racquet head above your hands, you set the racquet in position to hit the ball.

Ride the Roller Coaster: From the turn, the racquet will make a circular motion away from the body, keeping the racquet head above the hand.

Pet the Dog: Drop the racquet head below the hand, turning it parallel to the ground; as if you are petting a dog with your racquet.

Pull the String: Pretending there is a string tied to the bottom of the racquet, the string will be pulled toward the ball.

Turn the Doorknob: After making contact with the ball, the racquet will go from the hitting side to the non-hitting side of your body; like your hand is turning a doorknob.

Show Your Elbows: A completed swing will result in your elbows pointing toward your target.

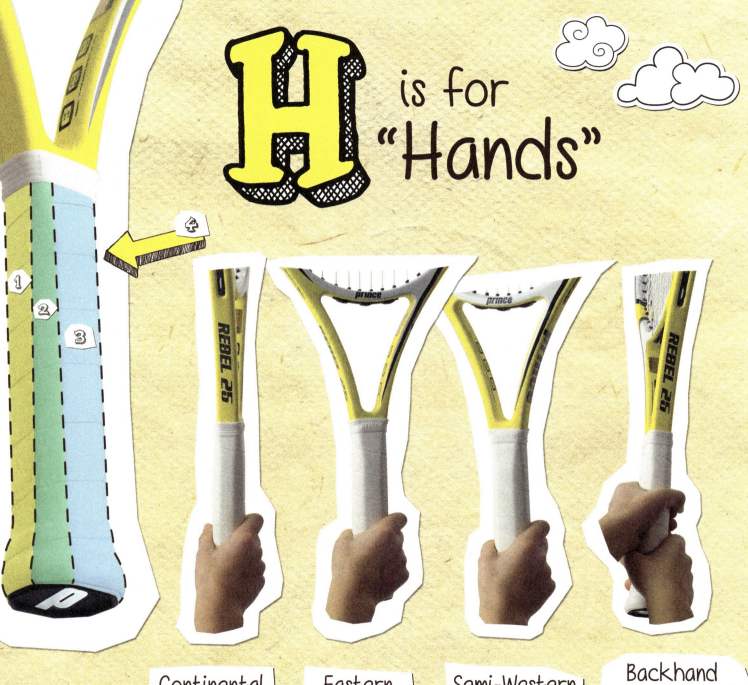

J is for "Just In Case"

When playing tennis, there are many things to keep track of; the wind, sun, the score. But just in case, make sure your bag is filled with extra grip, water, string, racquets, clothes, and anything else you might need while you're playing.

K is for "Keep the Score"

"What's the score?"

"The score is 40-15!"

In tennis, it is up to the players to keep score. So it is important that both you and your opponent are aware of what the score is.

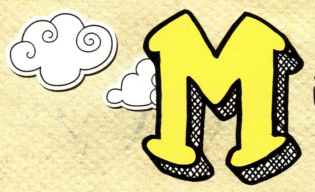 

M is for "Match"

A match in tennis is where two or four players are playing against each other. A singles match is between two players, a doubles match is between four players.

N is for "Net"

The net in tennis is the dividing line between the two halves of the court.

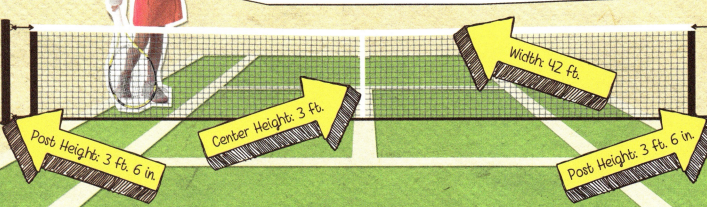

Post Height: 3 ft. 6 in.

Center Height: 3 ft.

Width: 42 ft.

Post Height: 3 ft. 6 in.

O is for "Open Space"

The area of the court that your opponent is not occupying.

Open Space

P is for "Point"

0 = love
In tennis, when you don't have any points, it is referred to as "love".

1 = 15
When you have one point, it is called "15"...

2 = 30
Two points is called "30"...

3 = 40
And three points is called "40".

3 to 3 = deuce

If the server wins the next point, it is called **ad in**

If the server loses the next point, it is called **ad out**

Q is for "No Quit"

No matter how far out of reach a ball might be, never give up.

S is for "Serve"

Phase 1

Phase 2

With both hands put in front of you, your shoulders should be pointing to the service box you are serving to. Make sure to stay relaxed and now is the time to call the score nice and loud!

Swing both arms back at the same time, creating a flow to the serve. As your hitting arm swings back, make sure it stays on the hitting side of your body. It's important to keep your palm down in Phase 2. As the hitting arm swings back the tossing arm will stretch to the sky to release the ball.

Phase 3

Trophy Position - From Phase 2, your hitting hand will raise up towards the sky to set the racquet in trophy position. The racquet will stay above the hitting hand while the tossing hand stretches toward the tossed ball.

Phase 4

Contact Point - From the trophy position your hitting hand will start to move forward and up to the ball. Make sure to hit that ball up and out in front of you for the best serve possible.

Phase 5

Follow through - Finally after you have hit the ball, your racquet will fall across your body. Make sure to keep your eyes up and forward as the point is ready to start now!

T is for "Tennis Court"

8 years old & under

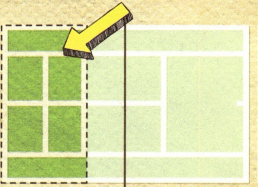

Court Size: 36 ft. x 18 ft.
Net Height: 2 ft. 9 in.

Red Tennis Balls
The slowest of all tennis balls. This ball also generates the lowest possible bounce.

9-10 years old

Court Size: 60 ft. x 21 ft. (singles)
60 ft. x 27 ft. (doubles)
Net Height: 2 ft. 9 in.

Orange Tennis Balls
This ball travels a little bit faster than the red ball and bounces slightly higher.

11 years old & up

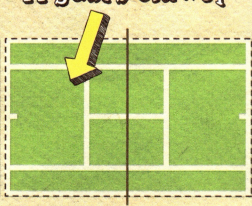

Court Size: 78 ft. x 27 ft. (singles)
78 ft. x 36 ft. (doubles)
Net Height: 3 ft (center)
3 ft. 9 in. (net posts)

Green Tennis Balls
This is the fastest and highest bouncing ball of all three tennis balls.

U is for "Up Against A Wall"

The great thing about tennis is that all you need is your racquet, a ball, and a wall to have fun.

whack!

Make a V for "Volley"

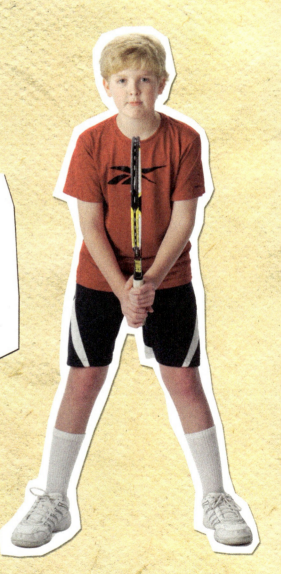

Remember these three simple rules for the volley:

- Keep your hands up and out in front of you
- Turn your shoulders sideways and remember to "Make the V"
- Push your hands forward without making a big swing and place the ball away from your opponent.

W is for "Winning"

After winning a match it is good to show emotion, but you want to make sure that in doing so you respect your opponent.

X is for "X Marks the Spot"

After hitting any shot make sure to move back to home base where "X marks the spot".

Y is for "Yourself"

During changeovers, make sure to focus on yourself rather than the things you cannot control.

To my Dad

for introducing me to the game I love and for always supporting me on and off the court

-KB

CPSIA information can be obtained
at www.ICGtesting.com
Printed in the USA
LVOW05*0956241115
462947LV00008B/11/P